HAUNTED
MONMOUTH COUNTY

HAUNTED
MONMOUTH COUNTY
Revolutionary Ghosts & Historic Haunts

LYNDA LEE MACKEN

Haunted Monmouth County
Revolutionary Ghosts & Historic Haunts

Published by
Black Cat Press
P. O. Box 1218
Forked River, NJ 08731
www.lyndaleemacken.com

Photo Credits: Library of Congress cover photo and pages 14, 15, 28, 34, 36, 48, 49, 50, 51, 56, 61, 65, 66, 69, 72, 76, 81, 96 and 99; U.S. Government photo page 22; Wikipedia/Ambrosiaster page 24; Village Inn by Blakefoto, licensed under the Creative Commons Attribution-Share Alike 3.0 Unported license, page 30; Deborah Lincoln grave by Joe Ryan page 83; Historic Walnford by Blake Bolinger, licensed under the Creative Commons Attribution-Share Alike 3.0 Unported license, page 85; Shutterstock page 87; all other photos by author.

ISBN 978-0-9829580-4-9

Printed in the United States of America by Sheridan Books, Inc.
www.sheridan.com

Book Layout & Cover Design by Deb Tremper,
Six Penny Graphics. www.sixpennygraphics.com

To my
nearest & dearest…

CONTENTS

INTRODUCTION...1

PORT MONMOUTH

SPY HOUSE...7

MATAWAN

BURROWES MANSION MUSEUM...13

ROSE HILL CEMETERY...18

MANALAPAN

MONMOUTH BATTLEFIELD...21

TENNENT

TENNENT CHURCH...25

ENGLISHTOWN

VILLAGE INN...29

FREEHOLD

COVENHOVEN HOUSE...33

FARMINGDALE

OUR HOUSE RESTAURANT...37

COLTS NECK

LAIRD & COMPANY DISTILLERY...41

SANDY HOOK

JOSHUA HUDDY'S HAUNT...44

SANDY HOOK LIGHTHOUSE...47

FORT HANCOCK ...49

NAVESINK HIGHLANDS

MAJOR CHARLES LEE'S SPIRIT...54

RED BANK

DUBLIN HOUSE...57

LONG BRANCH

PRESIDENT GARFIELD'S GHOST...60

WEST LONG BRANCH

MONMOUTH UNIVERSITY...64

Wilson Hall...65

Guggenheim Library...69

ASBURY PARK

STEPHEN CRANE HOUSE...71

WALL TOWNSHIP

HISTORIC ALLAIRE VILLAGE...75

IMLAYSTOWN

YE OLDE ROBBINS BURIAL PLACE...82

UPPER FREEHOLD

HISTORIC WALNFORD...84

CREAM RIDGE

HAPPY APPLE INN...88

ALLENTOWN

THE OLD MILL...92

IMLAY HOUSE...95

ACKNOWLEDGEMENTS...103

BIBLIOGRAPHY...105

INTRODUCTION

"I beheld the head of Washington, around about me glancing,
With a thrill of terror noting his silk-stockinged limbs were lost;
Lafayette's head disappearing left his shapely legs still dancing,
And I dreaded the misfitting of somebody's glorious ghost."
—ROSA VERTNER JEFFREY

There is no rest for the eerie in Monmouth County where history pre-dates the Revolutionary War. The region's historic landscape is dotted with a multitude of sites whose ghosts relate to the Battle of Monmouth, an important milestone in the American Revolution. Contested on June 28, 1778, the struggle featured British forces led by Lieutenant General Sir Henry Clinton against Continental forces commanded by General George Washington. Washington planned to attack the British before they reached New York. His campaign became a political triumph when his army forced a retreat. The general exposed himself to enemy fire which inspired and

1

motivated the American army to hold their own against the Brits.

In *The Scarlet Letter*, Nathaniel Hawthorne wrote:

"There is a fatality, a feeling so irresistible and inevitable that it has the force of doom, which almost invariably compels human beings to linger around and haunt, ghostlike, the spot where some great and marked event has given the color to their lifetime."

Hawthorne's words illustrate the disconcerting environment perceived at most battlefields. On the day of the Battle of Monmouth over 1,600 souls lost their lives. The energy of that day continues to seep through to the present for sometimes in the evening unexplained events occur on the battleground. Unknown spectral soldiers report for duty and stand guard in some area homes. At times, bursts of gunfire illuminate the woods or disembodied moans permeate the surroundings. One old legend recounts the ghastly appearance of skeletal Hessian soldiers ferreted out of the woods by a farmer's dog. Dressed in full uniform, the gauntly ghosts appeared willing to carry on the struggle they didn't seem to notice ended ages ago.

WASHINGTON AT MONMOUTH

Many theories exist regarding the reality of ghosts. It's suggested ghosts stay behind for a number of reasons—they are protesting an unjust end, they don't realize they're dead or they simply don't want to move on. Another hypothesis is the existence of parallel universes; both are invisible to the other yet exist side by side simultaneously. This might explain how individuals who have passed on to another realm can continue to appear in our world. Even though ghosts have been with us since ancient times no one can offer a definitive explanation for their existence.

4

Generally speaking, ghosts just want to be noticed—they want to be *re*-membered. Molly Pitcher, Captain Joshua Huddy and Major General Charles Lee all played a vital Revolutionary role. The residual energy of these iconic American personages remain in the area startling all who encounter their phantoms—an eerie experience they'll never forget.

At the Village Inn, the word "spirits" means more than a shot of whisky. No one knows this better than those who volunteer their time at the historic tavern where the sound of heavy disembodied footsteps ascending the stairs is unsettling. Stairways are high traffic areas and therefore hold a lot of energy. These established pathways store the energy of days gone by and somehow replay it for us to see, hear or feel in the form of paranormal phenomena. Several etheric characters in this volume are spotted on staircases particularly at Allentown's old mill, Sandy Hook's Officer Houses and Historic Walnford, among others.

Industry, such as iron and milling, flourished in Monmouth County during the 18th and 19th centuries. Communities developed around early gristmills. In Upper Freehold, Sarah Waln's spirit continues to survey her beloved property while James Allaire's apparition still grieves for his losses at the self-sustaining village that today bears his name.

Historic graveyards figure prominently in Monmouth County—especially the haunted ones. Some claim Matawan's Rose Hill Cemetery is New Jersey's most haunted burial ground and the Tennent Church graveyard is the otherworldly home for spectral soldiers, particularly one who unexpectedly met his end on neutral territory.

Historic homes creak and moan, as all old dwellings do, but a few in Monmouth County possess a little extra "boo!" The Burrowes Mansion and the Covenhoven House harbor faithful servants but Port Monmouth's Seabrook Wilson Homestead tops the list when it comes to hauntings. Let's start our armchair ghost tour at the notoriously spirited Spy House…

PORT MONMOUTH

SPY HOUSE

"Because I could not stop for Death,
He kindly stopped for me—
The Carriage held but just Ourselves
And Immortality."
—EMILY DICKENSON

The Seabrook Wilson Homestead is the most haunted house in Monmouth County—possibly the nation. Located at 119 Port Monmouth Road, the structure started out as a one-room residence built by Thomas Whitlock in 1648. Initially known as Strawberry Hill, the Spy House nickname evolved during the Revolutionary War. Historians debate the use of the building as a tavern during the conflict but most feel the house survived the Revolution by operating as an inn. As British mercenaries imbibed, the patriot innkeeper eavesdropped and shared

7

the enemies' secrets with the Colonials. This tactic resulted in the "Spy House" moniker.

Infamously haunted, the "woman in white" is one of the most dramatic manifestations ever reported. When seen, the apparition descended the attic stairs, proceeded into a second floor room and leaned over as if to straighten bedclothes. Oblivious to the present day surroundings, she turned and faded away.

The legendary landmark once boasted 22 active ghosts and hundreds of spirit sightings. According to a former township employee, the ghostly population includes, "Abigail and Peter, Lydia and Reverend Wilson, Captain Morgan, Robert…" The list goes on and includes a spectral British sea captain who peers through a spyglass toward the sea. Loud sobs emanate from the bedroom. This is Abigail's domain where she keeps vigil for her beloved's return with an expressionless stare. This is the same chamber where on July 4, 1975 a group of local boys observed the sewing machine door open and the foot treadle rotate according to the late paranormal researcher Hans Holzer in *GHOSTS, True Encounters with the World Beyond.*

Peter is Abigail's son whose phantom wears colonial-style shirt and knickers. When Gertrude Neidlinger curated the building as the Shoal Harbor Museum, Peter liked to play with the buttons used to activate the interpretive displays. He enjoyed meddling with visitors' cameras as well.

Psychics perceived the spirit of one of the former owners, Reverend William Wilson. They sensed him performing a funeral service in front of a bedroom fireplace. They also intuit a group of men strategizing in front of the first floor fireplace.

On a few occasions, Thomas Whitlock's spirit tagged along with visitors and actually went home with some of them. A former township employee said Whitlock craved attention and once accompanied her home where he drove her dog crazy. From time to time, the aroma of Whitlock's pipe tobacco wafted through the air and the phantom also pilfered cigarette packs yet always put them back.

Allegedly, the notorious pirate Captain William Morgan once commandeered the house and buried treasure underneath. The bloodthirsty buccaneer transacted dirty deals and tortures at the site. His nightmarish energy bled into modern times. Some youngsters observed Morgan's faceless phantom draped in a hooded robe and his terrifying bearded reflection in a mirror.

Psychic medium Jane Doherty used to conduct paranormal events on-site in order to educate the public and raise funds for historic preservation. The happenings were hugely successful and propelled the homestead to national fame. Spotlighted on the television show *Sightings*, the

U.S. News & World Report newspaper described the Spy House as one of the three most haunted houses in America. During one séance conducted at the house, Doherty contacted a spirit named Robert who claimed to be Captain Morgan's first mate. Robert exposed the existence of hidden tunnels leading from the house to the harbor. Sonar readings substantiated the possibility of tunnels. Doherty's psychic impressions revealed the presence of a trapdoor used during the Revolution by George Washington when he frequented the inn. Indeed a hatch existed where the psychic predicted and history substantiates Washington's stay across the bay in South Amboy.

One evening a volunteer left the building and witnessed children playing on the grounds. After a few confusing moments he came to realize their clothes befitted an earlier era—their outmoded garb a dead giveaway to their ghostly reality.

As one visitor approached the house via Wilson Avenue, he slammed on his brakes to avoid hitting a young girl who suddenly materialized in the street. The startling delusion offered a glimpse back in time. Historic records reveal a neighborhood girl named Katie died after being run over by a horse drawn carriage. Neidlinger alleged the apparition of a little girl holding a corncob doll appeared from time to time next to a tree on the property. Perhaps this is Katie's poor waif.

The Seabrook Wilson Homestead serves as the activity center at the Bayshore Waterfront Park. Docents conduct tours of the house which showcases bay ecology and local history including the American Revolution. The waterfront location affords panoramic views of the harbor and Manhattan's skyline. Dare to experience the possibility of the paranormal—perhaps gain a peek at phantom forms who figure prominently in the home's haunted history.

MATAWAN

BURROWES MANSION MUSEUM

"Left alone unto my dreamings, in that mansion old and haunted,
As the midnight hour was sounding came sweet echoes, soft and low,
From the ball-room up above me: it must surely be enchanted,
For footsteps there were gliding, gliding swiftly to and fro. "
—ROSA VERTNER JEFFREY

B uilt in 1723, the Burrowes Mansion became the home of grain merchant John Burrowes Sr. and his son Major John Burrowes Jr. At the time of the Revolution, Burrowes Sr. assumed the nickname "Corn King" as he traded mainly in grain. The Burrowes were a Patriot clan and proud members of the Sons of Liberty. In 1774, Senior Burrowes served as a delegate to the Provincial Congress that chose the delegates for the Continental Congress. After the Boston Tea Party, he actively supported the Boston patriots with food and money. When the first New Jersey militia formed they mustered in Burrowes' front yard.

John Burrowes Jr. served as a Major during the

war. His wife, Margaret, continued to live in the
house in order to hold down the fort, so to speak.
The Major returned to visit the homestead when on
furlough. Local Tories targeted Burrowes for capture
and actively scouted the house. During one of his
stays on May 27, 1778, they raided the Burrowes
property attempting to seize the Major. He escaped
their clutches but his father, John Sr., did not fare as
well. The invaders set several outbuildings,
including mills and storehouses, ablaze but spared
the house.

Throughout the attack, Margaret Burrowes brazenly stood her ground on the home's grand staircase. She boldly refused the demand of a British soldier to give up her shawl to staunch an officer's bloody wounds. The soldier retaliated by stabbing Margaret through the chest with his bayonet. It's alleged Margaret's steadfast specter still stands her ground on the stairway blatantly refusing to give up the ghost.

Margaret may not be the only wraith in residence at 94 Main Street. Docents hear disembodied footsteps and indistinguishable voices. In general, auditory apparitions are the most common event among supernatural experiences. When the Burrowes Mansion historian informed Patrick Kurdes and his Paranormal Activity Research Society (PARS) team about two young girls that haunted the living room, they heard movement on the second floor and then a young girl giggle. During the group's investigation, researcher Marina invited any resident spirits to touch her hair. Subsequently, Marina screamed and jumped off her chair after feeling someone stroke her tresses.

Various other ghost hunters captured several instances of electronic voice phenomenon (EVP). EVPs are the recorded voices of the dead not audible to normal hearing until they are played back on taping devices. Whispered declarations like, "Be gone," "Are you the Corn King," or "Your son is dead" are some of the EVPs recorded, according to Matawan Historical Society trustee Al Savolaine. Another recorded spirit voice in the attic said "help." The attic once served as the servants' quarters and it's where PARS photographed a ghost in the window.

The museum faithfully depicts an earlier time that's familiar to the spirits who once enjoyed the comfortable space. The site is gently spirited by a poltergeist who likes to move objects from place to place. Could this be Margaret's spirit putting things where she feels they ought to be?

A distant Burrowes relative, who at first wasn't aware of the house's mystic reputation, captured a light anomaly in one of the windows when taking a photograph. Margaret Burrowes' ghostly image she presumed and she's probably right.

ROSE HILL CEMETERY

Rose Hill Cemetery is the otherworldly stomping ground for specters unknown. The burial ground possesses the reputation as the "Most Haunted Cemetery in New Jersey."

Founded in 1858 on property once owned by Joseph Rose, the Victorian custom of the time shied away from churchyard burials and moved toward establishing garden-style cemeteries outside town parameters. Landscaped with hills, ponds and walkways the new fashioned graveyards became the first public parks where people could enjoy leisurely strolls and even picnics.

Rose Hill's topography offers views of Raritan Bay and the New York City skyline from its highest point. Legend says the Leni Lenape used the spot as a lookout as did Revolutionary patriots who used to spy on enemy ships from the vantage point then known as Fox Hill.

Rose Hill is the resting place of more than 3,000 souls and a number of gravesites relate to the famous 1916 shark attack in Matawan Creek. The horrifying event made national headlines and inspired the *Jaws* series of movies. Victims Lester Stillwell and Stanley Fischer are buried here along with Captain Cottrell, who first sighted the shark and rowed up the inlet to warn people.

William Stafford Little is interred at Rose Hill. Former President Grover Cleveland and future President Woodrow Wilson attended the well-connected politician's funeral. Even a Zombie is buried here—Zombie Hulsart that is.

The Matawan Historical Society hosts walking

tours of the property led by historian Al Savolaine. The tour guide has seen and heard the specters who roam the graveyard. He says sometimes he feels as if someone is standing right next to him, "almost breathing in my ear."

Ghost hunting groups consider the site a hot spot of supernatural activity. They experience battery drain on their equipment and capture audible and visual anomalies. Like Al the historian, some even see specters. Enjoy the historical society's guided walking tour of the site and see what manifests for you.

MANALAPAN

MONMOUTH BATTLEFIELD

"I am afeared there are few die well that die in battle..."
—KING HENRY V. ACT IV, SCENE I.

M olly Pitcher (1744-1832) was a nickname given to Mary Ludwig Hays who fought in the Battle of Monmouth. On the day of the fighting, Mary Hays doggedly carried water to soldiers and artillerymen, often under heavy fire from British troops. In the sweltering heat she incessantly answered their call for water to clean their guns and quench their thirst. "Molly, the pitcher" they yelled, "molly" being a generic term for a woman at the time. At one point in the mêlée she even draped a wounded soldier on her back and lugged him to safety. When temperatures reached over 100 degrees Fahrenheit, her husband collapsed. Mary assumed his place at the cannon and continued firing. For the rest of the day, she swabbed and loaded the gun. At one point, an enemy musket ball sailed between her legs and tore off the bottom of her skirt. Mary supposedly quipped something like, "Well, that could have been worse," and went back to work.

At day's end, General Washington asked about the woman he observed carting water, tending the wounded and comforting the dying during battle. To commemorate her courageous role, he issued Mary Hays a pension and a warrant as a non-commissioned officer recognizing her military service versus volunteerism.

Monmouth Battlefield State Park preserves the historical battleground offering a rural 18th century landscape of orchards, fields, woods, wetlands and the Craig House, a restored Revolutionary War farmhouse. The park's visitor center sits atop Combs Hill once controlled by Continental artillery. Every year, during the final weekend in June (or the weekend nearest to June 28), the 1778 Battle of Monmouth is re-enacted.

The intensity of the struggle left an imprint on the environment that somehow allows a playback of some of the day's events. One awesome ghostly tale that emerged from the conflict involves Molly Pitcher whose spirit appears to remain on duty. Some visitors to the park observed a woman in period costume offering water to the guests from the Molly Pitcher well memorialized at the site. One couple actually thanked the visitor center personnel for the authentic and thoughtful touch. The staff needed to explain that no one dressed as Molly Pitcher was enlisted to serve water to visitors. Imagine their consternation… They probably needed a drink after that!

TENNENT

TENNENT CHURCH

"Let's talk of graves, of worms, and epitaphs:
Make dust our paper, and with rainy eyes
Write sorrow on the bosom of the earth."
—King Richard II; Act III, Scene ii.

The peaceful setting at the 1751 Tennent Church obscures its place in our nation's early struggle for independence.

On Sunday morning, June 28, 1778, General Washington's army marched past Old Tennent toward cannon fire alerting them to battle. By evening the enemy was subdued—a much needed victory after one of the most grueling engagements of the Revolution.

The Tennent Church served as a field hospital during and after the Battle of Monmouth. At the height of hostilities, embattled American soldiers took refuge in the church where members of the congregation tended to their needs. As the injured lay suffering, musket balls bombarded the vulnerable sanctuary—some blasts breached the walls. These scars remained intact for patriotic reasons until it became necessary to repair the damage in order to preserve the building. The Tennent Church website goes on to say that as late as 1916, four cannon balls were dug up in the church ground during some grading operations.

On the day of the conflict, as one exhausted American militiaman, thought to be Enoch Coward, made his way to the shelter he stopped to rest on Sarah Mattison's grave. As Enoch sat in a war-induced daze an errant cannonball shot off his arm at the shoulder and broke the tombstone in half. He was hurried to the church and laid on a pew where his blood quickly drained the life from his body. The blood discolored the wood and *to this day* bloodstains are visible beneath the red velvet cushion covering the bench. For a while, the soldier's bloody handprint also marked the pew's book-rest until the wood was re-grained. Other pews are still scarred by the surgeons' saws.

They say poor Enoch's ghost is sometimes seen sitting inside the church on the pew where he died. He holds his head in his hands and weeps over his unexpected loss of life.

Over 100 known Revolutionary War soldiers are buried on-site. There is also a common grave of American fighters who died at the Battle of Monmouth—their number and identities unknown. British soldiers are also buried here. In addition to his presence in the church, Enoch's specter roams the graveyard as well. So do the spirits of other militiamen both British and American, their peaceful co-existence offer camaraderie beyond the grave.

ENGLISHTOWN

VILLAGE INN

"We meet them at the door-way, on the stair,
Along the passages they come and go,
Impalpable impressions on the air,
A sense of something moving to and fro."
—HENRY WADSWORTH LONGFELLOW

Long before paved roads crossed New Jersey, stagecoaches transported passengers to their destinations. Taverns, or "ordinaries" as they were called, were a necessity during the colonial era. Transportation modes of the day mandated the location of a tavern every few miles on main thoroughfares so that weary and hungry travelers could find refreshment. Taverns became public meeting places in early America. At a time when information traveled slowly, people congregated in taverns to hear the latest news. Broadsides were posted on tavern walls and, since mail and newspapers were often delivered there, the tavern keeper kept well informed.

Established in 1726 on the route between New York City and Philadelphia, the Village Inn on Englishtown's Main Street, played a significant role during the Revolutionary War. On the way toward their engagement with General Sir Henry Clinton's army on June 28, 1778, the American Militia passed the clapboard inn where General George Washington set up his headquarters.

Major General Charles Lee, who once served as a British officer, led 5,000 colonial soldiers as second-in-command under Washington during the epic Monmouth County conflict. Lee expected to be named Commander-in-Chief of the Continental Army. He felt more experienced than Washington so his resentment toward his superior simmered under the surface.

Washington ordered Lee to attack the enemy
however Lee withdrew his troops after only one
volley of fire. Lee retreated directly into Washington
and his troops as they advanced. The commander-
in-chief dressed him down publicly. General Charles
Scott said General Washington "swore that day till

the leaves shook on the trees." Lee was arrested and subsequently court martialed citing misconduct after Washington and Lord Stirling drew up the papers in the Village Inn. Jealousy flared, tempers raged and distrust erupted inside the tavern. Several months later, Lee was court-martialed and found guilty for his failure in leadership.

Undoubtedly, the intense emotions once generated inside the structure are imprinted there. Since energy cannot be destroyed it's theorized that sensations are somehow embedded on the environment. Consequently, the residual energy left behind by prior occupants can manifest paranormally. Author Daniel Barefoot in *Spirits of '76: Ghost Stories of the American Revolution*, shares the inn-side supernatural story about the Village Inn.

Apparently several Revolutionary War soldiers remain in residence. The sound of their phantom footsteps charging up the stairs is sometimes audible. Also, volunteers report inexplicable electrical phenomena. Lights turn on and off for unexplained reasons at the ancient pub.

Today the Village Inn is owned and operated by the Battlefield Historical Society. In addition to hosting ghosts, they conduct tours and special events throughout the year.

FREEHOLD

COVENHOVEN HOUSE

"All houses wherein men have lived and died
Are haunted houses. Through the open doors
The harmless phantoms on their errands glide,
With feet that make no sound upon the floors."
—Henry Wadsworth Longfellow

William and Elizabeth Covenhoven built
an impressive Georgian house in 1752-53.
The main rooms are furnished according to the
1790 inventory of William Covenhoven's estate
presenting a lifestyle showcase of a successful,
18th century farmer. British General Henry Clinton
occupied the house as his headquarters prior to
the Battle of Monmouth in 1778. The house is one
of several owned and operated as historic house
museums by the Monmouth County Historical
Association.

The Paranormal Activity Research Society, led
by Patrick Kurdes, investigated the home at 150
West Main Street after a docent witnessed a woman

in colonial clothing "float" across the living room and then disappear. Other odd experiences at Covenhoven included disembodied footsteps and the pages of the "sign in" book being turned. A home, or any place where people devote so much time, is potentially ripe for a haunting because the inhabitants' energy implants itself on the location. Former occupants feel comfortable here amid the familiar 200-year-old furnishings. How and why their energy manifests as spirits remains a mystery.

During their extensive investigation the team successfully captured three instances of spirit voices also known as electronic voice phenomenon (EVP). When Kurdes asked the spirits about the

British burning area homes as they approached Covenhoven's dwelling the eerie response sounded like "I don't know." The investigators also witnessed their REM POD react to an unseen presence. According to Kurdes, a REM POD is a device that radiates its own magnetic field. The gadget is extremely sensitive to field interference enabling invisible entities to stimulate the mechanism. When affected the alarm sounds and lights flash. No investigators were present in the room when the implement responded; the team's video cameras recorded the incident.

A few of the researchers experienced the sound of movement in vacant rooms as did this writer. Back in the day, I volunteered as a docent in the Covenhoven House for two days. The first day I received training, the second day I was left on my own to receive and inform visitors. No one showed up. No one tangible that is.

All alone, I wandered about the rooms acquainting myself with the particulars of the period furnishings and noting the colonial architectural details. Approaching the kitchen area, I began to feel nauseous, light-headed and dizzy. These symptoms indicate to me the presence of spirits. I distinctly heard people overhead moving about and conversing, although I couldn't understand what they said. The space above the scullery once functioned as the servants' quarters. I have to confess that being alone in haunted places unnerves me. After my experience all I wanted was the rest of the day to pass quickly. When my shift finally ended I said goodbye to the resident wraiths and never looked back.

FARMINGDALE

OUR HOUSE RESTAURANT

"Here I am, uncoated, unhatted,
Shirt all mildewed, hair all matted,
Sockets that each have royally
Fed the crow a precious eye."
—RICHARD GARNETT

During the American Revolution loyalists sought refuge from their patriot neighbors in the mysterious Pine Barrens. The feared terrain consisted of boggy swamps, sugar sand, pitch pine and white cedar. Colonists routinely avoided the territory frequented by runaway slaves, moonshiners and bandits along with the loyalists lurking in the thick shadowy tangle.

Jacob "Jake" Fagan is described as a miscreant who changed sides as often as the weather. As a member of the Second Battalion of New Jersey Volunteers, he actively recruited other loyalists. He reveled in robbing road travelers and plundering homesteads. The deaths of over 100 people are attributed to the villain. Fagan's gang hid out in the Pine Barrens where 30 foot tunnels dug in steep hillsides stored their ill-gotten gains.

Fagan's reign of terror came to an end in 1778 during a botched robbery at the home of Benjamin Dennis, a patriot officer. Fagan was wounded and carried away by his cronies. He died three days later and hastily buried. The next day some of his victims unearthed his corpse, wrapped it in tar-covered cloth and hung it near the highway. This ritual was commonly called a "degradation ceremony" according to Loyalist historian Stephen Davidson. Vultures "picked the flesh from its bones and the skeleton fell to the ground in pieces." Legend says the rogue's skull sat on display in a tree.

Lewis Fenton was another Tory robber plaguing

the Pine Barrens. A Freehold native, Fenton worked as a blacksmith before 1775. When he robbed a tailor's shop, he refused to return the plunder and instead opted for life as a fugitive. Fenton eventually joined Fagan's gang.

On June 5, 1779, Fenton and a fellow robber sought revenge on Benjamin Dennis, the man responsible for the deaths of seven comrades. They ambushed Dennis on the road to his Shrewsbury homestead. Inevitably, Fenton met the same fate as his other gang members. A contingent of Major Light-Horse Harry Lee's Light Dragoons, stationed at Monmouth County Court House, today's Freehold, captured Fenton in the boondocks and transported him to Farmingdale.

On September 23, 1779, Lewis Fenton hanged in front of Marriner's Tavern, Fagan's gang favorite meeting place. The tavern, now known as Our House Restaurant, still serves customers in Farmingdale to this day.

The landmark restaurant and banquet facility at 420 Adelphia Road is housed in the old tavern built in 1747 by George Marriner. The historic eating place is the second-oldest restaurant in Monmouth County. When all is quiet at the ancient eatery unusual happenings occur.

During renovations the owner noticed, with

some dismay, the ceiling fans and lights suddenly turn on by themselves. Another strange event took place one night as the proprietor deposited cash in the upstairs safe. The door to an adjacent small room, always kept locked, slowly began to open… then an inexplicable noise issued from within the space. The owner bolted down the stairs. Was Lewis Fenton's spirit attempting to rob the cashbox?

Since then no one likes to stay alone in the building. Disembodied footsteps echo overhead in empty rooms, the kitchen door creaks without moving and prints adorning the walls unexpectedly shift askew.

Is the hanged hooligan the culprit? Or his other menacing marauders? We've yet to know. Ghosts rarely harm anyone physically so if the spirit perpetrator is the outlaw Lewis Fenton, rest assure that in death he has been rendered harmless.

COLTS NECK

LAIRD & COMPANY DISTILLERY

"The boundaries which divide Life from Death,
Are at best shadowy and vague.
Who shall say where one ends,
And where the other begins?"
—EDGAR ALLEN POE

It's possible that Laird's Applejack, once known as "Jersey Lightning," was served at Marriner's Tavern. It was definitely dispensed at the Colts Neck Inn built by a Laird descendant in 1717.

Robert Laird founded the Laird & Company Distillery located in the Scobeyville section of Colts Neck Township. It is the oldest licensed distillery in the United States receiving License No. 1 from the U.S. Department of the Treasury in 1780 and remains the nation's sole producer of applejack, an apple brandy.

Robert Laird descended from William Laird who left his native Scotland and settled in Monmouth County around 1698. Most likely a distiller of scotch in his homeland, he began producing brandy with the most abundant resource available in his new country—apples! Robert served in the Continental Army under George Washington who requested and received Laird's recipe for "cyder spirits." Washington is the only outsider to secure the family formula.

Originally a farming community, Colts Neck Township is known for its large number of equestrian farms. It's worth noting that from 1837 to the early 1840s, inn proprietor and distiller Joseph Tilton Laird trained a racehorse named "Fashion." His son, Joseph, Jr., was the thoroughbred's jockey. Considered the best race horse of her generation, in

36 starts, the chestnut mare won 32 times. Fashion's victories garnered purses equivalent to over half a million dollars today. The winnings enabled the Lairds to move their distillery to the 22-acre Scobeyville property.

At one time, applejack was the nation's most popular drink. In the 1920s and 1930s, the Jack Rose cocktail was all the rage. The traditional libation contains applejack, grenadine and lemon or lime juice. The potion notably appeared in a scene in Ernest Hemingway's 1926 classic *The Sun Also Rises*.

Lisa Laird Dunn is the company's vice president and the ninth generation to share in running the family business. She grew up in the white Colonial clapboard house that functions as Laird & Company headquarters. Dunn's office is her father's childhood bedroom across the hall from her infant nursery. When things go missing in her office she blames "Uncle Joe." Joseph Tilton Laird III served as company vice president until he passed away in 1950. Dunn considers her workspace haunted because objects are routinely moved around or disappear altogether reappearing in a different place. Lisa regards Uncle Joe's poltergeist pranks a benign sign that he still shares an interest in the business.

SANDY HOOK

JOSHUA HUDDY'S HAUNT

"Sullen fires across the Atlantic glow to America's shore:
Piercing the souls of warlike men, who rise in silent night."
—WILLIAM BLAKE

During the American Revolution and well into the 20th century, military installations existed on the narrow spit of land called Sandy Hook.

Today Sandy Hook is part of the Gateway National Park Recreation Area. When the sun goes down on the barrier spit some say Captain Joshua Huddy's spirit roams the shoreline in an eternal search for his executioners—and with good reason.

The Highlands region played an important role in the Revolutionary War. Strategically important for both the British and Colonial armies, the region was constantly trafficked by troops from both sides.

Joshua Huddy served as a member of the Monmouth County Continental Militia. He actively, and successfully, pursued Tory gangs who plundered the area in search of American rebels. Huddy received a commission to operate a gunboat, *The Black Snake*, as a privateer in August 1780. Captured at his home in Colts Neck on September 1st of that year, the raiders attempted to burn down his house but Huddy surrendered instead. His captors tried to transport him across the bay to New York City, then British territory, but patriots on shore fired at the boat. The vessel capsized and Huddy escaped by swimming to safety despite receiving a bullet wound to the thigh. This incident infuriated the Loyalists and Huddy became a marked man.

On March 24, 1782, the enemy re-captured Huddy, this time during a raid of the blockhouse he commanded at the Toms River (then called Dover) salt works. Huddy thought he'd be exchanged for a Loyalist prisoner but when his captors received word that a Monmouth County Tory named Philip White had been killed, William Franklin, the last English royal governor of New Jersey, ordered Huddy's execution in retaliation. The Loyalists claimed Huddy's complicity in White's death even though they held him in captivity at the time.

Initially, Huddy was taken to a sugar house prison in New York City then transferred in irons to a guard ship at Sandy Hook where he was held until his execution on April 12, 1782. On that date, a party of Tories took him to the Highlands' Gravelly Point where he hanged. A party of patriots came upon their fallen comrade and carried him to the Old Tennent Church for burial in an unmarked grave. (A stone to his memory now exists next to the church, although the exact location of his burial remains unknown).

When Joshua Huddy's spirit manifests on the Sandy Hook shoreline he strides toward visitors as if to assess their hand in his death. When assured of their innocence his apparition turns and walks away eventually fading from view.

A monument to Captain Huddy is also installed at his namesake park at Bay and Waterwitch Avenues in the Highlands to commemorate the spot where he hanged.

SANDY HOOK LIGHTHOUSE

*"Well what is this that I cannot see? Ice
cold hands taking hold of me."*
—O DEATH, TRADITIONAL

Sandy Hook is also home to the 1764 Sandy Hook
Lighthouse. Situated just miles across New York
harbor, America's oldest lighthouse facilitated ship's
safety coming in and out of the busy port. The
unique octagonal design has withstood the test of
time, and even Hurricane Sandy (!), for 250 years.
A brick, three-story keeper's quarters exists nearby
featuring a veranda and two chimneys.

The British retained control of the lighthouse
for most of the Revolutionary War and a series of
skirmishes took place on the strategic peninsula.
In 1850, a skeleton was discovered in a secret,
underground passage beneath the keeper's house.
Nearly a century later, the bodies of four men and
one woman came to light at the base of the beacon.

The Sandy Hook Lighthouse was declared a
National Historic Landmark on June 11, 1964, the
200th anniversary of its first lighting. It still functions

as a safety beam for ships coming in and out of the Big Apple's harbor. It is lit 24 hours a day and maintained by the United States Coast Guard.

Some lighthouse visitors claim they felt an ice cold chill when someone tapped their shoulder while wandering the recreation area. Are British spirits still on guard defending their territory? Is the lonely entity the spirit of one of the displaced bodies unearthed at the site? Possibly it's the spirit of a lost soul looking for the light that will lead them home.

FORT HANCOCK

"With no hopes for companions, the ghost lets out a sigh
Trapped alone, forever, in a relic of an era gone by."
—DAVID MICHAEL CHANDLER

Numerous fortifications in defense of New York
harbor have existed on the six-mile peninsula. In
1899, Fort Hancock was established and thirty-four
buildings were erected in support of the installation.
An elegant row of Georgian Revival style officers'
houses still stand sentry at the water's edge.

Several years earlier Battery Potter was
constructed and outfitted with the nation's first and
only steam-lift gun battery, the most sophisticated

weaponry at the time. The wide variety of weapons installed at Fort Hancock range from cannons to Nike missiles.

Even though many of the gun emplacements and structures are disintegrating, a tour of the complex offers an enlightening experience and can elicit a ghost story or two. One chilling tale concerns a volunteer performing household chores in the old barracks, Building 102. He made up the bed and carefully smoothed the covers to create a neat appearance. Soon after, he noticed an impression appeared on the bed as if someone lay there. He straightened the bedclothes again and left

the room. He returned moments later and again found the indentation in the shape of a human body. When the volunteer shared this incident with his associates they offered similar experiences. The volunteers concurred the bedridden revenant could possibly be an ordnance accident victim from the weapons facility.

History House is a restored home open to the public on Officer's Row. Several years ago a park volunteer spent the night inside the old house. During the night she awoke to loud footsteps coming up the stairs. When she investigated the noise no one was found. The steps again resounded and this time they stopped at the foot of her bed. The woman felt chilled to the bone when a strange voice asked if she wanted some juice!

A visitor touring the house once resided in the dwelling next door. She claimed an officer committed suicide by hanging himself inside the home and alleged his ghost appeared to her regularly when she lived there as a child. Previous families fled when they witnessed not only the dead man's ethereal head floating in mid-air but a pair of disembodied shoes walking up the stairs. The tourist said since the spectral officer liked the woman's family he toned down his scary antics which made their co-habitation bearable.

For many years, a spectral soldier bearing arms stood at attention on the porch of Building 20 (Hartshorne Drive). The New Jersey Audubon Society now occupies the structure but reports no haunting activity.

NAVESINK
HIGHLANDS

MAJOR CHARLES LEE'S SPIRIT

"For him no minstrel raptures swell;
High though his titles, proud his name,
Boundless his wealth as wish can claim,
Despite these titles, power, and pelf,
The wretch, concentred all in self."
—THE MAN WITHOUT A COUNTRY

General Charles Lee's forsaken specter reportedly
roams the Navesink Highlands. The general is
most notorious for his seditious actions during the
Battle of Monmouth. George Washington ordered
him to attack but Lee retreated instead. Lee's
insubordination warranted arrest and a guilty
verdict at his court-martial in Brunswick, NJ.

Was Lee's decision a strategic mistake? He
believed himself outnumbered and felt retreat was
a reasonable tactic. The fact remains he disobeyed
orders and publicly disrespected his superior.

Some regard Lee's retreat as treason. While imprisoned by the British in March, 1777, Lee drafted a plan for military operations against the Americans. His allegiance to the patriot cause is suspect. He even failed to support Washington when he crossed the Delaware River on Christmas Day, 1776, by arriving late in Trenton.

Lee entreated Congress to overturn his guilty verdict without success. Failing this, he openly attacked George Washington's character. Lee's popularity plummeted.

On January 10, 1780, he retired to his estate in the Shenandoah Valley where he bred horses and dogs. While visiting Philadelphia two years later he was stricken with fever and died in a tavern. Fort Lee, New Jersey is named for him among other places.

Paranormal chroniclers Martinelli and Stansfield say Charles Lee's specter roams the Highlands dressed in a Revolutionary War officer's uniform notably without insignia or brass fasteners. His otherworldly attire reflects his "dressing down." The disgraced officer is reminiscent of a man without a country condemned to wander for all eternity. He played both sides of the fence and lost. No wonder his forlorn specter roams the Highlands with an eye toward Sandy Hook Bay as a gateway of release.

RED BANK

DUBLIN HOUSE

"Thus she spoke; and I longed to embrace my mother's ghost.
Thrice it slipped through my hands like a shadow, like a dream."
—HOMER, THE ODYSSEY

The dark, rich interior of the Dublin House
provides the perfect ambiance for a haunting.
The Irish pub is housed in a Victorian mansion that
started off in Middletown as a smaller structure.
Around 1840 it was transported across the Navesink
River to Red Bank and moved to a location lost to
history. In 1905, George Hance Patterson relocated
the house a second time to its present location at
30 Monmouth Street. These days, clairvoyants
contend his wife's spirit remains in residence. Mrs.
Patterson resided in the dwelling her entire life and
many certify her continued occupancy. Especially
convinced are the two Irishmen who own the pub,
Eugene Devlin and Sean Dunne. They consider Mrs.
Patterson's presence more of a companion then a
pesky poltergeist.

Contractors clearly perturbed Mrs. Patterson's postmortem patrols as they refurbished the building. Workers fell victim to several mishaps as they overhauled the house. Were the accidents related to Mrs. Patterson's presence? Hard to say, but Devlin and Dunn think so.

The woman's former bedroom exists on the third floor and now serves as an office where Patterson takes exception to the invasion of her personal sanctuary. One morning, upon Dunne's arrival, he found a metal shelf toppled over and its contents strewn on the floor.

The late T. J. McMahon was considered Red Bank's unofficial historian. The raconteur worked at the Dublin House for many years and he informed the owners of the resident wraith. After McMahon passed away, the owners dedicated a dining room to their comrade where they installed a glass cabinet to exhibit photos and other memorabilia. One day the display case crashed to the floor. Dunne blames Mrs. Patterson. After its replacement, McMahon's photo was found turned backwards. Is Mrs. Patterson peeved that Mr. McMahon's association with the tavern is memorialized and hers is not?

The invisible entity is such a part of the place that every morning Dunne greets the dowager with a pleasant "Good Morning!" Some more of the lady's ghostly antics include knocking over bottles, turning on lights and un/locking doors. Early on, as Dunne went to open a locked door he realized he left his keys downstairs. After retrieving them, Dunne returned to find the door now open. Undoubtedly, the ever-present Mrs. Patterson reached out from the great beyond to lend a helping hand to the man preserving her abode.

The Dublin House is the perfect place to enjoy a pint—and a poltergeist!

Seasonal lantern-lit walking tours of Red Bank commence outside the Dublin House. Contact Jersey Shore Ghost Tours, www.jerseyshoreghosttour.org, for additional information or call (732) 500-6262.

LONG BRANCH

PRESIDENT GARFIELD'S GHOST

"It is an unwise man who thinks that what is changed is dead."
—ANONYMOUS

In the late 1700s, Long Branch existed as a popular resort where actors, business leaders, health seekers and a sporting crowd frequented the grand hotels and elaborate summer cottages. Dubbed "the Monte Carlo of America," by the 1800s some of our nation's greatest dignitaries, including Mary Todd Lincoln, gathered here. By the first half of the 20th century, seven presidents vacationed in Long Branch as well.

Presidents Chester A. Arthur, James Garfield, Ulysses S. Grant, Rutherford B. Hayes, Benjamin Harrison, William McKinley and Woodrow Wilson all attended services at St. James Chapel (the Church of the Presidents) alongside wealthy summer residents. The rich and famous such as the Drexels, Goulds, Sloans and Vanderbilts enjoyed nearby palatial summer residences. The historic church is the only structure in Long Branch associated with all the presidents who vacationed in the seaside resort during its Gilded Age.

The Church of the Presidents stands at 1260 Ocean Avenue across the street from where the Francklyn Cottage (a 20 room mansion) once stood and the site where President James Garfield succumbed to an assassin's bullet.

On July 2, 1881, just six months into his term as president, Garfield prepared for a "working" vacation. He left the White House for the Baltimore and Potomac Railroad Station with his Secretary of State to board a New York bound train. As they passed through the station's eerily empty waiting area a slender man approached unseen. Charles Julius Guiteau, a soured and unbalanced federal job seeker, drew a revolver and fired twice. The president fell to the floor in a pool of blood.

Doctors arrived quickly. Their examination revealed a serious wound in the president's lower right back. The bullet lodged in his spine and triggered a fatal diagnosis. Although conscious, deathly pale and vomiting constantly, Garfield confounded doctors by living day after day. Despite valiant efforts, by late July, Garfield's health reached a crisis; his blood poisoning worsened—nothing could be done.

The wounded president was gingerly transported to Long Branch in the hope that sea

eight greenhouses, horse barn, cattle barn, poultry house, two-story palm house, bullpen, ram pen, sheep pens, pheasant pens, rabbit hutches, an icehouse, three workmen cottages and kennels for the six police dogs turned loose on the grounds every midnight. The self-sustaining enclave maintained a staff of 100.

Hubert, his wife Maysie and her sister Bertha led a lonely existence in their sumptuous digs. They were considered socially inept and despite constant invitations to lavish dinner parties, their old-moneyed neighbors gave the nouveau riche Parsons the cold-shoulder.

The 1929 stock market crash signaled the decline of Parson's fortune. Ten years later, the house went up for public auction. West Long Branch Borough, the sole bidder, purchased the estate for $100.

These days disembodied footsteps and pipe organ music still echo throughout the main campus building baffling all who discern the mysterious sounds. Staffers on the night shift hear indistinguishable conversations and the sounds of doors opening and closing when alone in the historic hall.

Most astonishing is a photo taken in the dining room sometime in the 1990s. The picture captured two transparent women dressed in maid uniforms tending to a modern day dinner party. Perhaps they stayed behind waiting for dinner guests to finally arrive.

In the Office of Special Events, an unseen presence sends chills up the spines of all the workers. According to the documentary, *Shadows of Shadow Lawn*, this eerie visit only occurs during times when staffers are preparing for a major event. Perhaps Mrs. Parson's spirit likes to have a hand in planning the well-attended parties thrown these days in her earthly abode.

GUGGENHEIM LIBRARY

Across Cedar Avenue from Shadow Lawn is the
Murry and Leonie Guggenheim Library built where
New Jersey's only vice-president, Garret A. Hobart,
once lived.

In 1903, Guggenheim appointed architects
Carrere and Hastings, designers of the New York
Public Library, to create a summer residence. The
Beaux Arts building received the Gold Medal from
the American Institute of Architects.

Murry Guggenheim died in 1939 but Leonie
continued to summer at her West Long Branch
mansion until she passed away twenty years
later. Many say Leonie's spirit glides along the

grand staircase every night—her filmy, phantom appearance witnessed by mystified campus police officers. The spirit's presence on the stairs may explain the detectible creaking often heard as well as the perceptible drop in temperature. Campus police even observed a female form wearing a white gown standing at a window in the middle of the night when they were certain the building was secure.

Many discern a definite presence that evokes unease among the library stacks. A sensitive French student became so distracted from her studies she had to leave the reading room because she felt certain an incorporeal entity observed her. Odd happenings occur in the computer room where cursors move on computer screens when no operators are near the monitors. Sometimes, inexplicable tiny triangles show up on the screens. Technicians cannot explain this mysterious glitch. From time to time, the scent of perfume is noticeable in the space where workers wear no cologne.

Most astoundingly, filmmakers inadvertently captured an awesome anomaly when filming the grounds for *Shadows of Shadow Lawn*. A garden statue, who some claim to be a likeness of Leonie Guggenheim, appears to blink and crack a slight smile. Expert analysis cannot explain the uncanny movement—to see the film is to believe it.

ASBURY PARK

STEPHEN CRANE HOUSE

*"A man had better think three times before he
openly scorns the legends of the phantoms."*
—STEPHEN CRANE

Stephen Townley Crane was born on November 1,
1871 in Newark, NJ. (Asbury Park was also
"born" in 1871, founded by James A. Bradley).
He was the youngest of fourteen children born to
Jonathan Townley Crane, a Methodist minister,
and his wife Mary Helen Peck Crane, a formidable
campaigner for the Women's Christian Temperance
Union.

After his father died in 1883, Crane's mother
purchased "Arbutus Cottage" at 508 Fourth
Avenue in Asbury Park. She enrolled her son in the
public school system where he wrote his first short
story. Crane later went on to work as a journalist,
filing stories from Asbury Park for a New York
newspaper. He was the first to chronicle Garden

State ghost stories with his 1894 essay entitled "Ghosts on the Jersey Shore."

He left Asbury Park behind when in 1892 he traveled to New York City. Three years later his masterwork, *The Red Badge of Courage*, was published to great acclaim in America and Europe.

During an elaborate Christmas party in 1899, which lasted several days, Crane fell ill while performing a ghost story for some of his literary friends that included Joseph Conrad, Henry James and H. G. Wells. He continued to write while taking the cure for tuberculosis in Germany's Black Forest. In 1900, at the age of 28, Crane died from the disease and was interred in the Evergreen Cemetery in Hillside, New Jersey. Unfortunately, his Newark birthplace was razed decades ago making his Asbury Park address the author's only remaining residence. The home is now a museum, performance and entertainment venue hosting readings, plays and classic movies.

Many deaths and hardships occurred in Arbutus Cottage and ghostly claims run rampant. Sightings of people in period clothing who appear then vanish away include a female apparition in the attic window and a man in Victorian clothing sighted on the second floor. It's chilling when objects move on their own in full view of dumbfounded witnesses. A fireplace trowel once flew off its rack and hit a young boy in the head. Hearing disembodied voices is startling along with the sudden inexplicable drop in room temperatures.

Members of the Syfy Channel's *Ghost Hunters* cast investigated the paranormal claims. The team diligently investigated and captured some anomalies yet in the end they could neither prove nor disprove the spooky allegations. Is the Crane house haunted? Some say yes... but no one can definitely say no.

WALL TOWNSHIP

HISTORIC ALLAIRE VILLAGE

"All day long, the town
Glimmers with subtle ghosts
Going up and down."
—D. H. LAWRENCE

Some claim a bog-iron production facility for pig iron operated here prior to the American Revolution although conventional history marks the Howell Works founding in the early 19th century. In 1822, James Allaire purchased the property as a resource for his Allaire Iron Works in New York City. At the time, his company led the manufacture of marine steam engines. He cast the brass air chamber for Robert Fulton's *Clermont* and sailed with Fulton on the steamboat's historic maiden voyage. The Howell Works also manufactured cast iron products. Allaire eventually transformed the site into a self-sufficient community, complete with housing and food supply for the workforce and its own post office, church, school and company store. The town even issued its own currency.

Bog iron production became obsolete by the increasing availability of iron ore so in 1846, the Howell Works furnace was extinguished. Allaire continued living in his village, while maintaining his New York business, until his death in 1858. When he died, the town's name changed to Allaire, New Jersey.

Today's Historic Allaire Village is a notable example of an early American company town. The settlement is also noteworthy for its ghostly inhabitants. In the Visitors Center for instance, psychics detect a strong, male energy. The entity is described as a nasty, angry man who wears boots. History records Benjamin Marks as the village supervisor who lived in one of the early row houses rebuilt on the original foundation. Marks disliked his job according to psychics who are able to read his energy. One morning as staffers performed their routine security check in the cellar they heard the sound of heavy footfalls. They cautiously approached the interloper and encountered the partial apparition of a man wearing boots! They suspect this startling effect stands as a postmortem visit from the tyrannical manager. Other mystifying manifestations in the building are electrical anomalies—lights, projectors, cameras and security systems usually go haywire for no reason.

Eric Mabius is an actor whose father became the museum director at Historic Allaire Village in the 1980s. The Mabius family lived on site and Eric and his brother considered the 330 acre park their playground. One foggy night they approached the "Big House," the founder's former residence. Dim security lights illumined the empty house as

Mabius peered through the window in response to the sound of inconsolable sobbing he heard coming from inside. He observed a tall figure dressed in funeral garb including a top hat. The man didn't seem "right," Mabius said. The apparition appeared inconsolable and turned his head toward Mabius looking him right in the eye. The sighting terrified the actor and troubled him for years.

Psychic medium Kim Russo hosts the documentary television series *The Haunting Of...* In 2012, Eric Mabius appeared on the program in an effort to obtain an explanation for his disturbing experience.

When a cholera epidemic hit New York City in 1832, James Allaire moved his family out of the town to his Howell village, but to no avail. His wife, Frances, perished from the disease and Russo's vision of a woman dying in an upstairs bedroom validated the sad event.

Russo also discerned the bodies of other cholera victims buried on the grounds particularly in the open quad area between the General Store and Allaire's mansion. For years the story of a lady in white floating over the area persisted at this location on the property. Psychics say the white lady admired Hal Allaire, the founder's son, even though she was bequeathed to a sailor. Her mariner never returned so her lingering spirit stays behind awaiting her beloved—or maybe her presence remains in pursuit of Hal's attention.

The death of his wife triggered a downward spiral for James Allaire. Shortly thereafter, a ship in which Allaire was part-owner, the *William Gibbons*, ran aground and wrecked. That same year, the Howell Works furnace blew and production temporarily ceased. The following year, America plunged into a severe recession and Allaire's uninsured steamboat *Home*, sank with the loss of 100 lives. The catastrophe damaged Allaire's reputation and practically wiped him out financially.

Another ghost in residence is Hal Allaire. He also haunts the Big House and his playful spirit enjoys taunting the costumed interpreters who work in the building. Hal lived at Allaire as a virtual recluse until his death in 1901. Without the funds to maintain the site the buildings fell into disrepair. The property became known as the Deserted Village of Allaire. The otherworldly Hal is a mischievous poltergeist who likes to move books and household objects. He apparently possesses a fondness for playing with candles as well. This proclivity became evident when Russo, who discerned Hal's presence along with his father's, posed questions to the men. The lighted candle on the table responded quite animatedly during the show.

Allaire Village is an epicenter of ghostly and paranormal activity. The village offers a spooky hayride, a haunted mansion, ghost stories, paranormal experts and tarot card readings around Halloween. All events are family friendly and not too scary. Just don't look in the windows of the Big House...

IMLAYSTOWN

YE OLDE ROBBINS
BURIAL PLACE

"O lost, and by the wind grieved, ghost, come back again."
—THOMAS WOLFE, LOOK HOMEWARD ANGEL

Between 1710 and 1714, several of Abraham Lincoln's ancestors resided in the sleepy village of Imlaystown. Mordecai Lincoln migrated to Monmouth County from his birthplace in Hingham, Massachusetts. His blacksmith shop still exists in Imlaystown and is listed on the National Register of Historic Places.

Mordecai Lincoln married Hannah Salter, the daughter of Richard Salter, attorney and wealthy mill owner. As it turns out the couple became the great-great-grandparents of Abraham Lincoln, 16th president of the United States. Hannah bore five children, one of whom they named Deborah.

Sadly, on May 15, 1720, the three-year-old passed away from a childhood illness. Her parents buried

their little girl in Ye Olde Robbins Burial Place, a
nearby cemetery established in 1695.

A monument on Monmouth County Route 524
marks the ancient graveyard and a path leading to
the overgrown burial ground. Known to history
as "Little Debbie," her tombstone reads: "Deborah
Lincon (archaic spelling) aged 3 years 4 months
May 15, 1720." An iron bar border frames the grave
to honor the girl's legacy as President Lincoln's
great-grandaunt.

A child's death is an unbearable loss and some
say the sadness endured by the Lincoln family still
lingers at Deborah's gravesite. Over the years locals
reported hearing mournful sobs emanating from the
burial ground, especially around the anniversary
of little Debbie's death. Some observe the strange
mirage of a ghostly horse-drawn funeral procession
entering the graveyard as well.

UPPER FREEHOLD

HISTORIC WALNFORD

"Next to the mill sits a lagoon,
that releases spirits each full moon.
The lagoon is but a shallow basin
but becomes paranormal on a certain occasion."
—ALAN SPENCER

Historic Walnford is the centerpiece of Monmouth County's 1098-acre Crosswicks Creek Park. In 1734 a village developed here around the gristmill, much like nearby Allentown.

In 1774, during the anxious days prior to the Revolution, Richard Waln relocated his family from Philadelphia to the seclusion of Upper Freehold. The Quaker merchant owned a wharf in the "City of Brotherly Love," giving him an advantage over competing area mills. Crosswicks Creek powered the mill and provided a transportation artery for market goods from Walnford to Philadelphia.

As a Quaker, Richard was a pacifist and refused taking sides during the Revolutionary War. This marked him as a Tory. He was arrested on July 21, 1777 and held behind English enemy lines on Staten Island, New York. Even so, he was allowed to visit his homestead. In August 1778, he petitioned Governor William Livingston and was permitted to remain home. An ardent abolitionist after the war, Richard actively participated in the New Jersey Society for Promoting the Abolition of Slavery.

Hessian troops passed by Walnford prior to the Battle of Monmouth. They repaired a bridge destroyed by patriots over Crosswicks Creek in the vicinity of the current bridge near the house.

Son Nicholas headed the Waln enterprise as full time farmer and milling merchant. Walnford reached its peak of production in the early 19th century when 50 people lived and worked on the 1,300-acre estate. When Nicholas died in 1848 his wife and daughter managed the operation.

By the close of the 19th century farming and milling practices were on the wane. Daughter Sarah Waln Hendrickson, who became a widow at age 41, saw the writing on the wall and realized Walnford's prosperity was slowly grinding to a halt. Business dwindled to milling corn and grain for area customers.

Sarah's nephew acquired the estate after her death in 1907 and transformed the property into a pastoral weekend retreat.

Today the 250-year-old village includes a corn crib, an 1879 carriage house, cow barn, grist mill and the 1773 Waln House where Sarah Waln's spirit still walks. Those who notice the specter describe her dressed in black. Her presence is mostly sighted standing atop the main staircase.

Another spooky anomaly is some cupboard doors refuse to stay closed. While visiting with spirit photographers, site supervisor Sarah Bent discussed this anomaly. Quite boldly, the door on a cabinet over the stairs near the servants' quarters *deliberately* opened in front of our eyes—not the slow movement of an off-balanced door. Photos taken reveal huge orbs and one photograph shot in the kitchen revealed a woman's face enclosed in the sphere. Is this eerie image Sarah Waln's spirit? Another snapshot captured misty ectoplasm swirling in the servant's quarters. Bent gave us a rare peek of the attic where photos taken revealed yet more orbs. New Jersey paranormal researcher Dave Juliano contends that an orb is an energy being transferred from a source such as batteries, heat energy, people, power lines, etc., to the spirit so they can manifest.

If Sarah's spirit counts as tenancy, the family's tenure here extends well into its third century.

CREAM RIDGE

HAPPY APPLE INN

"Here groves embowered and more sequestered shades,
Frequented by the ghosts of ancient maids,
Are seen to rise. The melancholy scene,
With gloomy haunts and twilight walks between."

—THOMAS GRAY

The community of Cream Ridge is home to the Happy Apple Inn a former mid-19th century stagecoach stop sandwiched between Trenton and the Jersey Shore. The current structure at 29 Imlaystown Road went up in 1904 after a fire destroyed the original structure.

As a side note, Richard Salter's mill and ironworks sits adjacent to the restaurant. Salter's son-in-law, Mordecai Lincoln, operated the iron forge, or "bloomery." Mordecai was the great-great grandfather of our 16th president, Abraham Lincoln.

A visit to this eatery elicited chat from a friendly bartender who spilled the beans about the occupant ghosts. For one, there's an ethereal tippler who enjoys sitting at the bar. No one knows his identity.

Another resident wraith is dubbed the "blue boy" because his ghostly image resembles the famous portrait *The Blue Boy* by Thomas Gainsborough. The boy's spirit appears dressed in 18th century fashion and two psychics claim his name is "John." John's apparition was first sighted peering through a window that overlooks the millpond. His presence is also perceived in the front room accompanied by his mother named "Grace."

Dawn Koby shared a lot of information about the spirited shenanigans occurring at the restaurant. In fact, she became a victim of a poltergeist prank when a stack of "guest checks" flew out of their cubby and hit her on the side of her face. Like most things paranormal that occur at the Happy Apple, she took it with a grain of salt.

The staff is sometimes plagued by phantom interference in the galley. Pots and pans rattle and other noises manifest when the spirits crave attention. One time, someone was up in the attic and heard a tremendous crash in the kitchen. They hurried down to see what caused the noise but found everything in perfect order. Something even brushes by the bus boys but they never see who caused the sensation. This anomaly usually mixes with a disembodied voice calling out, "Hey, you! Hey, you!"

Psychics also have something to say about the creepy doll propped in the ladies room. They claim the doll literally has the run of the place at night. Some say the ever-increasing dirt marks on the soles of her shoes attest to her midnight wanderings. Maybe she goes to visit the shadowy Civil War (?) era soldier who sleeps on the basement's earthen floor. (Maybe it's the dirt floor that gets her shoes grimier!)

Why is the inn so happily haunted? Most likely the reason is the restaurant's close proximity to water. Spirits need a power source from which to draw energy in order to manifest or manipulate the physical world. In this case, the millpond continues as a 21st century power outlet for the paranormal.

ALLENTOWN

THE OLD MILL

"Three spectral orbs arise from the pond,
ghostly avatars of men long gone.
Each ball of light flights right to the mill.
They penetrate the walls to resume their skill."

—ALAN SPENCER

Allentown is a small historic village located around the Mill Pond, along Doctors Creek and Indian Run. Originally settled in the 17th century, Nathan Allen constructed a grist mill and a cloth-fulling mill on the north bank of Doctors Creek between 1706 and 1715. Like most country villages in colonial days, Allen's Town grew around its mill. Main Street developed from an Indian path connecting settlements in East Jersey with those in West Jersey becoming the central thoroughfare from Amboy to Burlington during the 18th century.

Today's old mill building is Abel Cafferty's re-built gristmill (1855) on the foundation of Allen's original mill. Constructed of 300,000 bricks produced on-site, the gristmill operated for more than 250 years, up until 1963. Corky Danch purchased the landmark and its outbuildings in 1975. He focused on preserving the New Jersey treasure and offered an array of specialty craft shops, studios and a restaurant in the enterprise named the Allentown Feed Company.

Spectral vestiges still linger in the ancient structure. Upon entering the space a shadowy figure standing at the top of the basement staircase drew the attention of some visitors. It's surmised that the ghostly form is the spirit of a man who allegedly fell down the stairway to his death. Though it's subtle, the spectral energy permeating the mill convinced workers they shared their space with long-gone ghouls and attributed their unnerving perceptions to the fallen man's spirit. Feelings of being watched was especially strong in the basement where the company of an unseen presence pervades the place. There's a sense that something's not quite right…

Photos taken on the staircase and in the basement revealed unexpected orbs of light. Paranormal specialists contend these spherical artifacts signify the presence of spirits who willingly stay behind because they feel bound to their previous life or location for reasons unknown.

IMLAY HOUSE

"Far—as the East from Even—
Dim—as the border star—
Courtiers quaint, in Kingdoms
Our departed are."
—EMILY DICKINSON

James Henderson Imlay (1764–1823) graduated
from Princeton College and joined the Monmouth
County Militia during the Revolutionary War. As
a member of the New Jersey Assembly, he served
as speaker of the house in 1796. Imlay was elected
to Congress and served from 1797 to 1801. In 1804
and 1805, he performed the duties of Allentown's
Postmaster where he resumed his law practice.

Around 1790, Imlay commissioned the
exquisitely detailed mansion on Main Street that
bears his name. The original French wallpaper,
purchased in 1794, was removed and exhibited in
the American Wing of Metropolitan Museum of
Art in New York City. In addition, a replication of
Imlay's sitting room is installed at Winterthur, the
DuPont Estate in Wilmington, Delaware.

The building became a rooming house in 1900,
owned by Miss Emma Gordon. In 1936, Dr. Walter
D. Farmer converted the house into a hospital and
his office where he practiced until his death. The
building now houses retail shops, offices and a
private residence.

Before and during the Civil War, slavery
opponents assisted those seeking freedom.

Allentown's concerned citizens actively assisted the fugitives. In a compassionate gesture, John Imlay accommodated runaway slaves in the upstairs bedrooms of his home as opposed to the basement or other such second-rate lodging. Actually, a handmade shoe of old leather turned up in an upper floor hidey-hole. The material and workmanship is consistent with a 19th century slave-owned artifact and attests to their presence in the home's upper regions. This chapter of the house's history is further enhanced by the spooky story of three unearthly men playing a card game upstairs. The ghostly remnants of their pastime is residual energy from the past informing the present.

Before relocating his shop called "Two Country Ducks" to Smithville, Robert Koch used to operate the retail business in Imlay's building. He said that as a local television crew filmed a commercial at the site, the displeased spirits reacted to the invasion by throwing things off the shelves. They also displaced candles and other objects by moving them around from one place to another. At one time a high school girl working in the shop heard a noise in the fireplace. She approached the hearth, and thinking it might be a small animal, gently poked inside the firebox with a fireplace tool. Whoever or whatever made the sound grabbed the implement and gave it a good pull! The rattled young woman quickly exited and subsequently resigned.

Georgette Keenan is the long-time proprietor of "Necessities for the Heart" gift shop located in the Imlay House. She determines a lot of people have passed on in the house because of its history of slave habitation and hospital tenancy. She says "psychic" shoppers find the store's energy intriguing and the often get the "willies." One paranormally sensitive customer noticed the place was "loaded" with spirits and found it difficult to enter the back room.

When Georgette first opened her business, she presented a tea-themed shop. Working alone at night in the building she often heard clanging and banging noises coming from adjacent rooms. She said the sounds reminded her of little boys wrestling and pushing each other into walls. Growing up with two older brothers, I agree with Georgette's assessment of the commotion. Every night before they went to bed my brothers always caused a ruckus which elicited threats from my father to be quiet... or else, and pleas from my mother to go to sleep. Georgette said this happened frequently, occurring at the same hour of night each time. She assumes the evanescent culprits are some of Imlay's sons whom he adored.

A spectral young woman seemed to take up residence on the porch. Passersby would sometimes spot a figure in the front window. A former shopkeeper's daughter constantly saw the phantom female darting quickly to and fro. The wall between the porch and Georgette's shop was always, unnaturally, freezing cold. She said that more than a few times as she held tea tins in her hand while showing them to customers the container would fly out of her hand. This anomaly occurred only in that spot in the shop.

In the past, one particular vendor experienced bizarre events. During her monthly visits, the representative's computer went down yet outside the shop the device worked perfectly. While taking inventory of the handbags the purses would plop off the shelves and fall on her head! She'd say, "Stop bothering me—you're dead!" When she at last finished scanning the merchandise for inventory purposes the computer erased all her work. Georgette and her gals very often find a handbag in the *middle* of the floor. This anomaly is not merely the result of a pocketbook falling off the shelf—it's too far away from the display to be a coincidence.

Twice a year, when daylight savings time began and ended, the staff needed to reset all the clocks and watches that were for sale in the shop.

On several occasions they found this task already accomplished by unseen hands.

Office Manager, Marianne Newman, is a no nonsense kind of gal. One time, as she straightened a box of eyeglass holders displayed on a chair, Marianne spotted someone in the mirror that was also placed on the chair. She turned to greet the female customer but... *there was no one there.*

Although the paranormal pranks have petered out somewhat, Georgette feels the playful, phantoms haven't left. I sense the ghosts harbored in the Imlay House consider this place a safe house as did the former fugitives on their way to freedom.

ACKNOWLEDGEMENTS

I am indebted to the following individuals who
generously and graciously shared their stories
and other relevant information that served
to enliven (so to speak!) the ghostly tales.
I truly appreciate your helpfulness.

Georgette Keenan & Marianne Newman
Necessities for the Heart

John Imlay

Robert Koch
Two Country Ducks

Dawn Koby & Kyle Westendorf
Happy Apple Inn

Sandy Epstein
Guggenheim Library

Patrick Kurdes
Paranormal Activity Research Society

Sarah Bent & Maggie Stroehlein
Historic Walnford

Bill Van Pelt & Chef Keith Warner
Black Forest Restaurant

Sincere appreciation to my talented graphic
designer Deb Tremper, founder/owner of
Six Penny Graphics. Like the monks of old,
Deb's creativity illuminates the printed page.

Special thanks to Maryann Way for always
taking time and care with my manuscripts.
Mare's thoughtful suggestions
help bring it all together.

BIBLIOGRAPHY

Antonucci, Nicole. "Rose Hill Cemetery holds lessons in Matawan history." *The Independent*, October 25, 2012.

Barefoot, Daniel W. *Spirits of '76: Ghost Stories of the American Revolution*. John F Blair, Publisher; October 31, 2009.

Chesek, Tom, "Ghosts In The House 'Turn of the Screw' at Monmouth U." *Asbury Park Press*, June 18, 2004.

Considine, Bob. "Dark Shadows at the Shore." *Asbury Park Press*, October 25, 2008.

Conte, Stephen, "Lincoln's New Jersey Roots." *WEIRD NJ*, Issue #13, 1999.

D'Amico, Jessica. "Area haunts play hosts to reported ghosts." *The Hub*, October 17, 2013.

Davidson, Stephen. "The Pine Barrens: Jacob Fagan's Gang." *Loyalist Trails UELAC Newsletter*, October 12, 2012.

DiIonno, Mark. *A Guide to New Jersey's Revolutionary War Trail*. Rutgers University Press, 2001.

Fryckstaedt, Olav W., Ed. *Stephen Crane: Uncollected Writings*. Upsala Press, 1963.

Ghost Adventures. "George Washington Ghost." Season 9, episode 3, March 1, 2014.

Harrison, Karen Tina. "Jersey Lightning." *New Jersey Monthly Online*, July 13, 2009.

Hauck, Dennis William. *Haunted Places, The National Directory*. Penguin Books, 1996.

Heimbuch, Jeff. Allaire State Park. http://theweirdusmessageboard. yuku.com.

Henderson, Helen & Matawan Historical Society. *Matawan and Aberdeen, Of Town and Field*. Arcadia Publishing, 2003.

Hladik, L'Aura. *Ghosthunting New Jersey*. Clerisy Press, 2008.

Holzer, Hans. *GHOSTS, True Encounters with the World Beyond*. Black Dog & Leventhal Publishers, 2004.

Kelly, Kathy A. *Asbury Park's Ghosts and Legends*. Paranormal Books & Curiosities Publishing, 2010.

Macken, Lynda Lee. *Ghosts of the Garden State*. Black Cat Press, 2001.

_____. *Ghosts of the Garden State II*. Black Cat Press, 2003.

_____. *Ghosts of the Garden State III*. Black Cat Press, 2005.

_____. *Ghosts of the Jersey Shore*. Black Cat Press, 2011.

_____. *Ghosts of the Jersey Shore II*. Black Cat Press, 2014.

Martinelli, Patricia A. & Stansfield, Charles A. *Haunted New Jersey*. Stackpole Books, 2004.

Matawan Historical Society. "Burrowes Mansion, Haunted by Matawan's Past." *Matawan-Aberdeen Patch*, October 4, 2012.

Mills, W. Jay. *Historic Houses of New Jersey*. J. B. Lippincott Company, 1923.

Monmouth County Park. *Historic Walnford* brochure.

Moran, Mark & Sceurman, Mark. *Weird N.J. Your Travel Guide to New Jersey's Local Legends and Best Kept Secrets*. Sterling Publishing, 2009.

Nesbitt, Mark. *More Ghosts of Gettysburg*. Thomas Publications, 1992.

Perrotto, Patrick and Tom Hanley. *Shadows of Shadow Lawn* (DVD). Hawk TV, 2005.

Pierce, Arthur D. *Smuggler's Woods*. Rutgers University Press, 1960.

Reynolds, Joe. "Sandy Hook is a Weird & Creepy Park." *Atlantic Highlands Herald*, November 9, 2009.

Roberts, Russell & Youmans, Rich. *Down the Jersey Shore*. Rutgers University Press, 1997.

Rockwell, Anne. *They Called Her Molly Pitcher*. Alfred A. Knopf, 2002.

Sitkus, Hance Morton. *Allaire*. Arcadia Publishing, 2002.

Stives, Ruth Calia. "Imlay House may be part of Underground Railroad." *Examiner*, May 7, 2011.

Sudol, Karen & Moore, Kirk. "Jersey Shore Haunts." *Asbury Park Press*, October 3, 2006.

Staab, Amanda. "A Haunting Encounter: When Ghosts Berate The Unsuspecting." *NJ Monthly Online*, September 12, 2012.

Stansfield, Charles A., Jr. *Haunted Jersey Shore*. Stackpole Books, 2006.

Symmes, Rev. Frank Rosebrook. *History of the Old Tennent Church*. Printed by G.W. Burroughs, 1904.

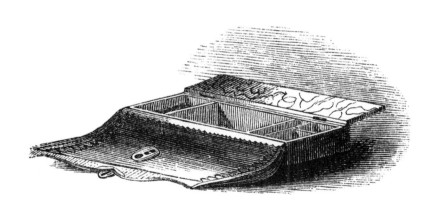

WEBSITES

Borough of Allentown, NJ: www.allentownnj.org

ClipArt ETC: http://etc.usf.edu/clipart

Crossroads of the American Revolution: www.revolutionarynj.org

Early History of West Long Branch: www.westlongbranch.org

Garden State Ghost Hunters: www.gardenstateghosthunters.com

Haunted New Jersey: www.hauntednewjersey.com

The Historic Village at Allaire: www.allairevillage.org

Jane Dougherty: www.janedougherty.com

Monmouth University: www.monmouth.edu

New Jersey History's Mysteries: www.njhm.com

Our House Restaurant: www.ourhouserestaurant.net

Paranormal Activity Research Society: www.parsinvestigations.com

Revolutionary War in New Jersey:
www.revolutionarywarnewjersey.com

The Shadowlands: www.theshadowlands.net

Small Town Gems: www.smalltowngems.com

The Stephen Crane House: www.thestephencranehouse.org

Tennent Church: www.oldtennentchurch.org

Wikipedia: www.wikipedia.org

Other Haunted Titles by Lynda Lee Macken

Adirondack Ghosts

Adirondack Ghosts II

Adirondack Ghosts III

Array of Hope, An Afterlife Journal

Empire Ghosts, New York State's Haunted Landmarks

Ghost Hunting the Mohawk Valley

Ghostly Gotham, Haunted History of New York City

*Ghosts of Central New York

Ghosts of the Garden State

Ghosts of the Garden State II

Ghosts of the Garden State III

Ghosts of the Jersey Shore

Ghosts of the Jersey Shore II

Haunted Baltimore

Haunted Cape May

Haunted History of Staten Island

Haunted Houses of the Hudson Valley

Haunted Lake George

Haunted Lake Placid

Haunted Long Beach Island

Haunted Long Island

Haunted Long Island II

Haunted New Hope

Haunted Salem & Beyond

*(originally published as *Leatherstocking Ghosts*)

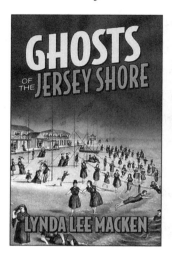
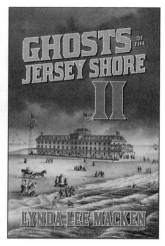

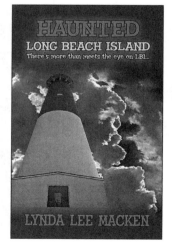

In Grateful Remembrance
of Patriots Who, on Sabbath June 28, 1778,
Gained the Victory Which Was the Turning Point
Of the War for Independence.